FAIRY TAIL

3

HIRO MASHIMA

FAIRYTAIL
Contents

Chapter 14: _Titania_

Are you running away, Erigor?!!

CRASH

Dammit!! He's gone into the other block!

You two go after him!!

Natsu!! Gray!!

Hrrm...

If you can combine your powers...

...not even Erigor should be able to stand against you!!

Huh ?!

HYUUN

I'm going, too!!! I've got a score to settle with the pink-haired guy!!

WHOOM

I'll stop them and be right back!!!

KYUUUUU

Eisenwald Member:
Rayule

Look at that! Rayule and Kage have gone all belligerent!

I don't get it! Dancing with these little girls looks like so much more fun!

They're doing it to help the mission! That's a lot more important than your likes and dislikes!

Once we take care of these guys, we'll go after Erigor, too.

Yeah!

Eisenwald Member:
Karacka

Eisenwald Member:
Byard

LUCY! COME BACK TO REALITY!!

Being so cute is a curse, right?

You slime!

WHOOSH

Wait, wait! That's only after they do a fairy strip show for us!

Let's capture 'em and sell 'em!

It'd be a shame to kill them!

What can two little girls do?!

But they're two pretty little girls, huh?

HYA HA HA HA

H-How... can this woman... requip so quickly?!!

Requip?

An axe?!!!

To change out one of those weapons for another is to "requip."

Magic weapons are much like your celestial spirits, Lucy. They are stocked in a different dimension and called forth.

Weapon Cache in Another Dimension

There are still this many left?

Erza?

Huh?

Actually, Erza's truly amazing point comes next.

Really? That's amazing!

Natsu... Gray... Lucy... The rest is up to you!

You, too, Happy.

I knew it! This is what I get for speeding too fast in that magic four-wheeler.

ZWOOO

Fire and water can't combine to do anything!!

It's impossible!!

We're supposed to combine our strengths?!

Don't make me laugh!!

TMP TMP TMP TMP

Hey, quit imitating me!!!

I can defeat Erigor on my own with no problem!!!

She wants to decide everything on her own!!!

Erza spouts too many orders!!!

You understand, Natsu?!

This is a good place to split up!

Which way?

Humph!

We're up against a real fool who's trying to release dangerous magic on the world!!

Once he's found, he's got to be pounded into the ground!!

He won't get off that easy!

He was dumb enough to pick a fight with Fairy Tail!

And I'm going to burn him to a crisp for it !!!

Humph!!!

!!!

GWUK

Hehn!

Nothing!!! Now get going!!!

Hm?

TMP

Don't die, okay?

So they're going to use that to broadcast their murdering curse music!

I'm not going to stand for it!!

Tsk!

TMP TMP TMP

So that's it!!! If he wants to broadcast Lullaby...

...then Erigor has to be in the room with the PA equipment !!!

Broadcast?!!

STUDIO

HEH

If he wants to broadcast the sound, this is the only place with the equipment to do it, right?

Why isn't he here?!

Isn't broadcasting the song their goal?

W-Wait a second...

It's weird. Somebody should be here!

WHOOSH

You're standing in the way of our plan!!

Your... instincts are too good to allow you to live!

So there are some ulterior motives behind this, huh?

Geez! I know you don't work for a living, but don't you have anything better to do?!!

22

Chapter 15:
Fairies in the Wind

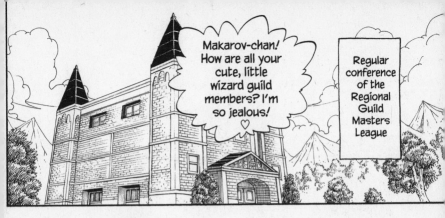

Makarov-chan! How are all your cute, little wizard guild members? I'm so jealous! ♡

It's all well and good to be active, but your people tend to overdo things, don't they?

Eeek! You're such a perv! ♡

YEAH YEAH

Yeah!!! That was my new member Lucy! She's great! Especially around the chest region!!!

ZEHEH HEH HEH

I heard all about how your guild members gave some local despot a spanking!

Quatro Cerberus Wizard Guild Master: **Goldmine (♂)**

Blue Pegasus Wizard Guild Master: **Bob (♂)**

Makarov-sama! I bring you a letter from Mirajane-sama.

Hm?

Honestly! ♡ You know it's not right to lay a hand on your wizards!

Hya hya! The things I want to pound on are Lucy's jugs!!!

There are people on the Council who are worried that Fairy Tail is going to pound down an entire town someday.

24

Erza has formed a team with both Natsu and Gray!

Of course Lucy and Happy are on the team, too.

!!!

And while you were out, the most wonderful thing happened!!

Oh?

What do you guys think? *This* is my guild's poster girl!!

Isn't she the sweetest thing?!!

OOH

おおおっ

Master, thank you for your hard work at the regional meeting.

I wanted to pass the news on to you, so I'm sending this letter. See you!

FFT

If you ask me, I think it's the most powerful team that Fairy Tail has ever put out!

...

Well? Isn't that wonderful?

Just make sure no disasters occur before then!!!

The meeting ends today. Tomorrow I go back...

Wh-What's going on?!! They really *could* pound down an entire town!!!

FAIRY TAIL
Please!!!

!!!

WHUMP

Makarov!!!

Wh-What's wrong with him?!

Eeeek!!

They couldn't have been wiped out by terrorists, could they?!

The army went in, but nobody's come out!

What's going on in there ?!

And this wind! It's so strong!

Look!! Somebody's come out!!

It's better than seeing them all die.

H-Hey you!!! Why are you saying that?!! Are you trying to incite a panic?!!

KARANG

...but there's always that one chance in ten thousand that we can't. You'd better evacuate.

Of course we're going to do everything possible to stop it...

You should know that everything I have just said is true.

...will find himself dead!!

Anybody who stands between us and our mission...

You don't have a mission anymore!! If you want to broadcast Lullaby, this is the only place to do it from.

WHOOSH

TAK

TAK

Erigor was holding Lullaby, and he isn't here! So I don't see why you all took this station!

You don't think you can take on a building full of the most powerful wizards in the world?!!

Ha ha!!!

GM GM GM

That's right!! Nobody will be able to stop it now!!

And you fools might have stood in the way, but you can't leave this station!!

ゴゴ GM GM

Erigor *will* get away with it!!

Those old farts don't know anything!! And there's no reason why they wouldn't listen to a little music!!

!!!

We've been injured and insulted, and now *we* don the judges' robes!!! And everything will vanish before us!!!!

Chapter 16:
Capture Kageyama!!

It's the meeting with all those old guys!! That's who they're trying to play Lullaby for!!!

Eisenwald's real target is the station at the end of the line!!!

And while we're wasting our time here, Erigor is getting closer and closer to the Masters meeting.

If we try to force our way through it, we'll be turned into ground beef!!

Yeah!! I saw that before I got here!!

But right now, some wind wall has this station pinned down.

I've heard most of that from the ones down here.

Hm?

!

Stop that. They know nothing.

EEE!!

GANCH

H!!

Don't these guys know how to turn the wind wall off?!

45

If so, he can dispel the wind wall!!!

Is he a dispeller?!!

Remember that Eisenwald has one among them called "Kage"!!!

He's the one who broke the wards to Lullaby all on his own!!!

We must hurry and capture this Kage!!!

TMP

Tsk!

S-Sorry...

You heard, right?

GWIP

Karacka...

How long are you going to keep hiding?

Huh?!

No... You've got an easier job...

G-Give me a break! I'm no good defending other people!!

They're after Kage. You have to go!!

GWOOOO

-SHIVER-

-IVER-

Wh-What?

Say, why don't we go back to where Erza is?

!!

Aww!! We've lost track of everybody!!

Aye.

TWITCH

Wh-What would Erza do to me...?!!

You're willing to ignore Erza's orders, huh?

I can hardly believe it! You're amazing, Lucy.

I don't want to see what you'll look like when Erza gets through with you.

This is *Erza* we're talking about!

Erza told us to follow that guy!!

Hmp!

Hmp!

Where are you hiding?!!!!

Come on!!!!

BAKOOM

バツワーン

．．．

Next!!!

Next!!!

D-Doesn't he know what doors are for?

He's the most destructive guy I've ever seen...

50

Say you under-stand!!

Fuu...

Glegh!

I...

I under-

Kage!!!!

!!

Chapter 17:
The Virgin Magic

Kage!! Hang in there!!!

We need your powers!!!

Hey!!!

Ah...

Uh...

Aah...

I don't believe this!!! Dammit!!!

Eee!!

SUPOKK

Eeeee!!!

Wasn't he...

...one of you...?!

Aye.

I-I think we'd only be in the way.

Maybe I'll fly!

I've even regained most of the power I lost when I made the magic wind wall!

The town of Clover where the Guild Masters are gathering...

...is close!!

Those old cretins who stole our work...our authority!!

Just you wait!!!

HYUUUUU

I'll kill you all using Lullaby!!!!

HYUUUUUU

The Death God decrees punishment!!!!

HYOO

...is the Guild Masters meeting?!!

So what Erigor is after...

GWOOOO

I'm gonna bust through this thing!!!

WHA CHEE

Idiot! Brute force won't do this job.

Natsu!!

WHUMP

If it could, I'd have done it already.

WHOOSH

But we've got to act fast!

Can't your magic freeze it or something?

ZUGMGMGMGM

Ngwoooo!!!!

Kh!!

You're just going to tear yourself apart!!!

H-Hey, wait a second!!!

Stop that!!!

Dammit! What do we do now?!!!

What?!

GWIMP

I said stop!!!

Yeah, but... Normal humans will die if they go in there.

They can't breathe!

I was able to go from one place to another through the celestial spirit world, right?

Eh?

That's right!!! Your celestial spirits!!!

Cut the long explanations and do it!!!

I'm explaining that it can't be done!!!

...at the very least, you will need a celestial wizard outside the station for it to even be possible.

In other words, if you want to get out of here through the celestial spirit world...

Besides, the Gate only opens in the place where the celestial wizard is.

Everlue's...

...key?

Back then, it was Everlue's key, so we were lucky!!

One more thing! Humans passing through the celestial spirit world is a bad breach of contract!!!

SHF

Something I was trying to remember when we came to your place!!!

Lucy!! I just remembered !!!

Wh-What?

Ahhhhh !!!!

SHF SHF

This !!

Isn't that...

... the key to Virgo ?!!

Virgo...

You mean that gorilla of a maid?!!

We don't have time to waste discussing stupid things like this!!

What are you talking about?

Ehh?!!

No! Virgo herself wanted me to give it to you!

You shouldn't have that!!! It's wrong to just grab it and...

GRIP

That's really nice to hear, but we shouldn't be talking about it right now! We have to think of a way to get out of here!!

...came to us?!

That thing...

She came to our house to ask about it.

She said that the contract was broken the minute Everlue was arrested.

And she said that this time she wanted to create a contract with you, Lucy!

I thought that maybe she'd be able to help get us out under the wind wall.

Virgo was able to dig beneath the ground.

......

Be quiet!!! Cats should meow and not be heard!!!

But...

Hand it over!!!

Honestly, why didn't you say that in the first place?!!

Really?!! You *can* be useful at times, Happy!!!

Is that true?!!

What?!!

I...one who connects the path of the celestial spirit world to our own...

...command you who I call to pass through your Gate.

Because you were pinching me, Lucy.

Virgo!!!

Open!!! Door of the Virgin Palace!!!

Huh?!

Did you call, Mistress?

BLINK

DMGWOOO

"Lost weight"?!! She's a completely different person!!!

Please forgive my prior actions.

You've lost weight!

Lucy... I should have guessed.

Hmm? She's pretty cute.

Your last Master was higher placed and a more skilled wizard.

So...

Keep the side comments to yourself!!

I am the loyal servant of my Master or Mistress. I will take the form that my Master or Mistress wishes and faithfully do my work.

U-um... That look of yours...

That's about right.

Then, "Princess."

What's "right" about it?!!

Never mind! Just hurry!!

As you wish, Mistress.

Very well, Dominatrix.

Not that, either!!!

We are in a hurry!!! Can we save contract negotiations for later?!

Let's not use "Mistress," okay?

ZUBON

WHOOSH

And so, I shall begin!!!

Whoa!!!

She went underground!!!

Good!!! We can use that hole to get out!!!

GONG

OWW!!

Good work, Lucy!!!

It'll leave a bad taste in my mouth if he dies after fighting me!!

What are you doing, Natsu?!

GRMP

OOF

Hurry!!!

This wind's awful!!

Cover up your own!!

Princess!! Others may see your underwear!!

BWAA

We're out!!!

Huh?

WHOOOOO

Happy's gone, too!

!

Where's Natsu?!

You're too late. There's no way you'll ever be able to catch up with him now.

We... we've won...

Chapter 18:
Fire and Wind

KATAK

KATAK

KATAK

KATAK

So we have to pay compensation, huh?

KATAK

KATAK

KATAK

KATAK

This isn't... the same magic four-wheeler car that we rented, is it?!!

Eisenwald seems to pay a lot of attention to details, and one of them was completely destroying the car we came in.

S-So why did you bring me along...?

We only borrowed it!!! According to Erza, anyway.

KLNCH

Heh... You went and stole another car, huh?

No!!! I'm asking why you saved me!!! I'm the enemy!!!

So we're bringing you to a doctor in Clover!!

You should be thanking us!!

What did you expect?! There was nobody left in town!!

Wait, Gray!!

You want to die? I can kill you if you want.

Oh, man! Do you have to be so depressing?!

Oh, I get it! I'm your hostage to be used as a bargaining chip in your negotiations with Erigor.

It won't work. He's completely cold-blooded. He won't trade me for anything.

Heh heh.

All you guys should think of the future a little.

Life or death isn't the only way to settle things, you know.

!!!

KAKLOK

Erza
!!!

Forgive me. It's all right.

GUNSH

Eeeek
!!!

...
!!!

My eyes are glazing over.

I knew I was using too much magic power....

HAH

HAH

Hey!! I had a good line back there!! Don't make it worthless!!!

DU-GLUP

Huhhh?!! That's sexual harassment!! Gray, kill him!!!

Can't you go on a diet and slim down that huge rear end?!

Just long enough for me to get us there!!!

Natsu... Stop Erigor where he is...!!!

GRRRNNN

If you don't stop him, all the Guild Masters in the entire region will be dead!!!

87

Come on!!

I'll do you a favor and burn up that dangerous flute of yours!!

The magic wind wall...

And what happened to Kageyama and the others?!!

I only had a little farther to go to get to where all the old men were!!!!

BWOOOHH

SHLIPP

It isn't fair!!! Come down and fight!!!

Flittering around up there!!!

Dammit !!

Is this what Fairy Tail calls a wizard?!!

What kind of idiot is he?! It's like nothing he does is planned!!

So from now on, I'm going to get serious.

I may... have underestimated your power.

I'm all fired up!!

You do the same!

HYOOOOOOO

Storm mail !!!

Chapter 19:
Impossible! Natsu Can't Win!

Natsu!!!

Natsu!!!

It's impressive that his corpse is still in one piece.

He wasn't a bad fighter for being so young.

Come on, get up!!!

!!!

What's this...

SHVR

SHVR

...Lullaby crap...

Guided to you by Lullaby's tune!!!

But you won't feel too lonely, kid. I'll be sending the old men to be with you soon.

If you want the old men's heads so much, you should take them on in a fair fight!!!

You're still alive? !!

That's impossible !!!

If you don't have the guts to fight them, then you don't have the right to be here!!!!

GONG

Why can't I get close to the guy?!!!

I don't accept it!!!!

KRICK

KRICK

GWOO

It looks like your emotions translate directly into magic power.

Still, your magic is unusual.

GM GM GM

BWOOGH

BWOOGH

KRICK

Ngaaaaa!!!!

Wh-What's this?! The wind surrounding Erigor has changed direction!!

GWOOOOO

No... There's no way that a kid like him could use ancient magic.

I remember there being some mention of that kind of magic in ancient times.

Emotional flame...?!!

Aaaaaaaaa!!!!

Aa!!
Aa!!
Aa!!
Aa!!

What do you think of that, Happy?!!!

GONG

It's what I'd expect from Natsu the Salamander!

Aye!

Wow! Natsu's memory is worse than a cat's!

GRAK

You said how I can't win, and then something or other about Erza, right?!!!

A cat's memory isn't the best in the world.

Now, about what you said back there...

TAK TAK

But the winner was you, Natsu!

It's because you're amazing, Natsu.

Ha ha ha ha ha ha!!!

Oh, right !!!

Well... whatever.

But why did my last attack get through to him?

Heh heh heh...

GHWOOOOOO

oooo

Chapter 20:
To Live Strong

ズガガガガ゛゛
ZUKANG KANG KANG KANG

Natsu!!!

Oh!

You guys are late!! It's already over!!

Aye!

Why *my* clothes?!!

Lucy, give me your clothes!

You have no right to say anything!!

Look at you!! Half nude except for a scarf! Like some kind of exhibitionist!!

Putting all that aside, you did well, Natsu.

This puts the Masters out of danger.

We should ask the Masters how to dispose of the flute.

While we're here, we should go to the Guild Masters meeting place and report what has happened.

Clover isn't far away at all.

Good... It looks like the meeting hasn't ended yet!!

HAHH

HAHH

HAHH

POIT

TWITCH

ZLMM

そろそろ...

At this distance, they should all hear Lullaby with no problem!

Heh heh heh... Finally! The time has come!

Wha—?!

Hya hya hya hya hya hya hya!!!

GLUNK

I have to hurry and find out where those three are going!!

An entire town could be wiped off the map!!

Oh no!! This is no time for jokes!!!

KAFF KAFF

KAFF

. . . . . .

Tsk!! Why am I fated to bump into flies wherever I go today?!!

Makarov...!!! He's Makarov, the Master of Fairy Tail!!

Get yourself to a hospital!!

You leave as fast as you can, too!

HUP

Be sure to listen well!

"They act so high and mighty no matter what poor quality wizards they call members!!"

"All of the official guilds are pathetic!!"

"The first part of it will be to kill all of the Guild Masters in the area!!!"

WOOOO

"They stole our work from us, and we will get our revenge on the world of magic!!!"

"And it's these fools that sent us into darkness!!"

"You aren't getting your right to work back by doing that!!!"

"Kage... Please... We need your power."

"All you guys should think of the future a little."

"He was in your guild!!! He was supposed to be one of you!!!!"

All I have to do is play it!!

I should just play it...

Nothing will change.

And that'll change everything!!!

Weak people will always be weak!

ZHKK

Humans basically start out weak!

But not everything weak is evil.

Guilds exist because it's frightening to be alone!

That's why we have friends!!!

We band together and march in step in order to live strong!

A lot of people are clumsy and bump into walls.

They may be taking a roundabout way of doing things...

...strength will naturally well up.

...but if they keep on walking and trust in tomorrow...

And if you laugh and decide to live strong...

THUNK

I've lost!!

Old man!!!

Hey, old guy!!!

Master!!!

Chapter 21:
The Most Powerful Team!!!

ZUSHUNK

144

145

That monster is Lullaby itself! In other words, it's living magic.

That is what Zeref's magic is!!

I don't understand what happened! How did a monster come from a flute...?!

Who could have imagined that his dark legacy of hundreds of years ago could appear in our world today?

Zeref the Black Wizard! He was the most evil wizard in the history of magic.

Zeref?!! But Zeref was from ancient times!!

Living magic...

I've made my decision!

Now...which of your souls should I eat first?

147

The power to put a form to magic.

Maker magic?

He can perform maker magic that large in just an instant ?!!

He's fast !!!

SHIVER

There's also magic that steals form away.

Ice make...

...lance !!!

*FIRE DRAGON'S GLEAMING FLAME

KA-WHOOM

You were so cool !!!

That was great !!!

Exactly right!!! Amazing, aren't we?!! Ha ha ha!!!

Oh, you!! We have to get you to a doctor!!!

Right?! ♥

Hya... aa...

!!

I don't know what to say!!! Hya hya hya hya hya!!!

Yes.

Well, I don't understand the whole story yet, but it looks like we owe a debt to Fairy Tail.

SNEAK

!!!

Hm?

KRUMMBBL

Noooo!!! Our meeting place...

It's reduced to rubble !!!!

Ha ha!!! Aren't you impressed with how completely it's destroyed?!!

Master, please forgive us... We've made you lose face...

You're one of the people who needs to be arrested!!!

Fine!! Just leave that to me!!!

Arrest them!!!

TMP TMP TMP

Don't worry. They'll never invite me to another meeting again anyway!

162

Chapter 22:
Natsu vs. Erza

The official meeting place of the Council, Era.

Even with Eisenwald put down, it hasn't done anything to solve the root of the problem.

There are still as many dark guilds as stars in the sky.

But how?

Then we must begin the plan to eradicate them all!

The blame will fall not only on them but rise up to those in higher positions as well.

And how were they able to get their hands on such dangerous magic so easily?!

We can't let anyone bring out more of Zeref's magic like they did this time!

They took down an entire guild with only four or five people. I'd say that's amazing!

...but this time, they've saved us.

I know that Fairy Tail has been a thorn in your side...

I understand how you would rather not accept it, but it is a fact.

Gak...

Urk...

ざわっ

CHATTER

165

If all of those Guild Masters had been murdered by Lullaby, the situation would be infinitely worse.

Many of us in this room would have lost our heads over it.

Magic Council Member:
Siegrain

I'm fed up!!! Their gratuitous violence is enough to make me hang my head!!

Foolishness!!! Do you intend to cast blame in this hallowed hall?!!

Why don't you just accept the facts, and give them a word or two of praise?

Eisenwald's attempted terrorist attack on a meeting of Guild Masters made the national news.

I still can't believe that I could have been in the middle of such a big event.

GWIP

Today, I think I'll do some shopping.

But even so, life goes on, as it always did.

At times, though, I think back to those events, and my heart starts to pound.

According to rumors, that Kage guy and nearly all of the other members of Eisenwald were arrested.

Well, that's only natural.

One scary thing was that Erigor was never captured.

I worry about what I'd do if he came to get revenge on Fairy Tail.

TA-DAH!!

Fairy Tail's strongest team of Natsu, Gray, and Erza...not to mention the cat and myself...are here waiting for him. ♡

But everything's okay!!

So Mama, please don't worry about me.

This guild is the best!

I'm doing just fine!

Sigh!

THOK

P.S. Please keep all this a secret from Papa, okay?

For this place, rent of 70,000 Jewels is cheap!

Sure, it's fun being on a scary, exciting adventure...

...but it's at home that I can really relax!

You found yourself a good place, Lucy.

Breaking and entering!!!!

JAAN

Go home!!!

Wait a second! You got it wrong!! I stripped *before* I came here!!

VSH

Gwaa!!

And don't go stripping in other people's houses!!!

THWAK-

I thought you might have forgotten, so I came to remind you.

It's going to happen today.

"It?"

See? You did forget!

Natsu mentioned it even before we set out, remember?

CHATTER

CHATTER

CHATTER

CHATTER

YAAAH

YAAAH

Huh?

You, Natsu, and Erza, of course! You're Fairy Tail's top three, aren't you?

"Most powerful team?" What's that all about?

But if two members of the most powerful team face off against each other...

Now you made her cry!

Oops! Mirajane, you said it...?!

That's stupid!! Who'd say something like that?!

There are a lot of incredibly strong fighters in Fairy Tail!!

I'm one of 'em!!

I'd go along with you if you said that Natsu and Gray were pretty manly, but I can't listen to you say "most powerful" and stay silent!!

And for the strongest man, there's Mystogan or Laxus.

And we can't discount the old man, either.

But there's no real doubt that Erza is the strongest woman.

173

After a long time, I get to test my strength!!!

GWOOOOO

This will not be play-acting for me, either.

That would cut Natsu's power by at least half!!!

It's the *fire empress armor!!!* It's armor that protects against fire magic!!!

Erza is making this fight serious !!!

Hit me with everything you've got!!!

DWOO

175

I'm no good at this!! I don't want either of them to lose!!

You're more pure-hearted than I expected.

I've never seen such a faithless cat!!!

ODDS

Natsu | Erza

Do you mind if I bet on Erza instead?

POIT

I was hoping you'd wear that!!!

Your fire empress armor...

GWOOGH

Now I can fight you with everything I've got and have no regrets!!!

I am an envoy from the Council!!

To all, do not move from this spot!!

During the occasion of the Eisenwald terror case...

...as a suspect in eleven counts of property damage...

Don't his looks even register on you guys at all?!

Why would he be here?!!

A messenger ?!!

The Council ?!!

TO BE CONTINUED

The Early Design Work for the Fairy Tail Bar

We've only been able to fit a small selection onto these pages (and only those that were rejected). Actually, several dozen sketches were drawn for it. As I'm sure you'll see if you look at the manga pages, the interior has gotten much simpler. There are all sorts of odd characters all over the place, so we went with a simple interior so as not to distract from them.

I ANSWER YOUR QUESTIONS!

Among all of the letters that I've received from fans, the question I am asked most often is this:

"What's the relationship between *Siegrain* and *Seig Hart*?"
Yes. *Siegrain* is that guy on the Council, right? And Seig Hart...isn't even in this manga!! He's a character from my previous manga, *Rave Master*! Anyone who hasn't read both wouldn't even understand this question, so I'll explain briefly. Seig Hart has a name similar to Siegrain, and they have similar faces. Moreover, they both use magic. So those who know my previous work well would like to know their relationship. Very well. This is the answer.

They are completely unrelated!! (Utterly)

My previous work, *Rave Master,* and *Fairy Tail* are two unrelated universes. Even if Siegrain seems like a character you may have seen before, he is a completely different character. Basically Siegrain is a character I designed as a bit of fan service for those readers who have also read *Rave Master*. But he's a different character with a different personality. So, if you don't know who Seig Hart is, no problem! It's just that Seig Hart is a cool guy, and a good guy as well. Siegrain, this time, will probably turn out to be a bad guy. I still don't quite know, though...

Happy's Job (Little) 2

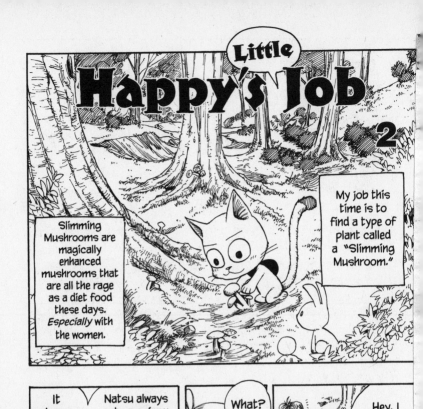

Slimming Mushrooms are magically enhanced mushrooms that are all the rage as a diet food these days. *Especially* with the women.

My job this time is to find a type of plant called a "Slimming Mushroom."

It always happens!!

Natsu always eats a poison mushroom called "Laughing Bamboo."

What?

Hey, I know one thing.

Who cares? Let's just search!

Your words and actions don't seem to match!

I'd never do anything that stupid!

What are you talking about, Happy?!

MUNCH
GOBBLE
CRUNCH

Natsu, are you all right?!!

See?!! There it is!!!

Nnnnnn !!!

Hm?

I'm even more surprised !!!!

POP

That sure surprised me!

DOOOM

Are you depressed over that?!!

?

But it isn't Laughing Bamboo...

But the request sheet also said to be careful of look-alike mushrooms.

No doubt about it!! It's exactly like the picture on the request sheet!

Are you sure this is it?

There it is!!!

はっ
CLAP

When did I ever look like a bratty, hungry little boy?!!

Bratty?

Because you're looking kind of hungry.

Why does it have to be me?!!

So you should do a taste test, Lucy.

If we bring back the wrong one, it'll soil the name of Fairy Tail.

Hm ?!

Nnnnn !!!

Wait, Happy!!! You shouldn't do that!!!

It could be poisonous!!! Spit it out!!!

But Lucy, you said there was no doubt about it.

はっ MUNCH し

POP

Gyaaaaa !!!

Hm? Wait a second...

That isn't your biggest problem, is it?!!

The joke loses all its power the second time around!!!

No fair!!! Natsu gets all the good jokes!!!

Urk!

Haven't your mushrooms grown a bit?

The End

AFTERWORD

In the afterward of volume 2, I asked what people would like to see in bonus pages, and the most frequent response was "I'd like to see a Fan Art section!" Wow!! You people really love to draw, huh? As someone who likes to draw myself, I'm very happy to hear it! And so, I guess I'll just go ahead and make a Fan Art section!! Clap clap!! Hm... Let's see... As a name for the section, how about, "Fairy Tail d'Art"? Hm... Too long, huh? And I get the feeling that I've heard it somewhere before... Oh! I know!! "Guild d'Art"!! How about that?

The idea is this: Inside Fairy Tail, there's a corkboard, and people post art there instead of requests for missions. What do you think? What's that? You don't care how I package it? Well, anyway, I hope everyone sends drawings into the Guild d'Art. Draw whatever you want, but make sure it's with black pen. Even if you want to shout, "I can't draw!!" send in your drawings anyway. This isn't about good drawings or bad drawings. Guild d'Art is about fun drawings (depressing drawings are good, too). Just bring it!! I'll figure out some kind of present for those lucky few who get into the publication.

Send your art to:

Kodansha Comics
451 Park Ave. South, 7th Floor
New York, NY 10016
publicity@kodanshacomics.com

Okay, I'm going to draw, too!! Oh, in the next *Fairy Tail*, Natsu and the group take on a job they really shouldn't take!!

When you send letters, postcards, and other mailings, personal information such as your name, address, postal code, etc., will also be delivered to the author. Please keep that in mind when you send mail.

Also, please keep in mind that while Kodansha Comics will make its best efforts to deliver your fan letters to Mashima-sensei, a reply to your letter cannot be guaranteed.

About the Creator

HIRO MASHIMA was born May 3, 1977, in the Nagano prefecture. His series *Rave Master* has made him one of the most popular manga artists in America. *Fairy Tail,* currently being serialized in *Weekly Shonen Magazine,* is his latest creation.

Translation Notes

Japanese is a tricky language for most Westerners, and translation is often more art than science. For your edification and reading pleasure, here are notes on some of the places where we could have gone in a different direction in our translation of the work, or where a Japanese cultural reference is used.

General Notes:
Wizard

In the original Japanese version of *Fairy Tail*, you'll find panels in which the English word "wizard" is part of the original illustration. So this translation has taken that as its inspiration and translated the word *madôshi* as "wizard." But *madôshi*'s meaning is similar to certain Japanese words that have been borrowed by the English language, such as *judo* (the soft way) and *kendo* (the way of the sword). *Madô* is the way of magic, and *madôshi* are those who follow the way of magic. So although the word "wizard" is used in the original dialogue, a Japanese reader would be likely to think not of traditional Western wizards such as Merlin or Gandalf, but of martial artists.

Names

Hiro Mashima has graciously agreed to provide official English spellings for just about all the characters in *Fairy Tail*. Because this version of *Fairy Tail* is the first publication of most of these spellings, there will inevitably be differences between these spellings and some of the fan interpretations that may have spread throughout the Web or in other fan circles. Rest assured that the spellings contained in this book are the spellings that Mashima-sensei wanted for *Fairy Tail*.

Requip, page 11

The Japanese used a word that isn't standard Japanese, *kansō*, that is made of the kanji that means "change" and another kanji that means "equipment." Since the Japanese word was coined just for *Fairy Tail*, I decided to make up an English word that will convey the same concept.

Titania, page 15

The kanji translates out to "Queen of the Fairies," but the katakana pronunciation guide next to the kanji reads "Titania." This seems to be an obvious reference to the queen of the Fairy Kingdom, Titania, who is found in Shakespeare's comedy *A Midsummer Night's Dream*, among other classic fantasies.

WakuWaku Land, page 52

The Japanese word *waku waku* means to be excited, and it seems a fitting word for the name of a theme park. Northeast Asia is second only to North America when it comes to the popularity of amusement parks. Japan has about thirty large amusement parks with attendance of more than a million guests per year, and an equal number of medium-sized parks with an annual attendance of 500,000 guests. Overall, the industry accounts for seventy-five million attendees and $1.5 billion in annual revenues—about 30% of U.S. attendance figures in a country that's only as large as California. (Figures circa 1998.)

Orochi, page 53

The mythological beast's full name is Yamata no Orochi (the eight-forked serpent), and it comes from the book of Japanese myths, the *Kojiki*. Orochi is said to have eight heads and eight tails. The god Susanoò, who had descended to Earth, helped save the last of the eight daughters of an earthly god from being devoured by the beast. Susanoò had the god brew saké, which had been refined eight times, as bait and place the saké in eight vats. When the serpent was drunk, Susanoò started hacking away.

Meow and not be heard, page 75

I know Lucy's line doesn't make any sense, but this is very close to a direct word-for-word translation of the Japanese. It doesn't make any logical sense in Japanese, either, and that's probably the reason for Gray's reaction.

Dominatrix, page 77

"A woman with a whip" is shorthand for an S&M dominatrix in Japan. In Japanese, they are called *joò-sama*, which is one of the Japanese words that mean "queen." But, although the word "queen" is apparently also used in western S&M circles, it does not immediately conjure up the image of a "dominatrix" to the average English-speaking reader. For that reason, this translation uses a more direct term.

Storm Bringer, page 94

Although Erigor's attacks have kanji in the Japanese original, the kanji have a pronunciation guide (*furigana*) that was written in the characters usually reserved for foreign words (katakana). And the pronunciation written was the English words "Storm Bringer." The same

holds true for Erigor's later attack names (with the exception of Emera Baram below).

Emera Baram, page 107

Most of Erigor's spells are in English, but this one wasn't. Since the pronunciation guide was written in katakana (see the above note), it was obvious that the pronunciation was supposed to be foreign sounding. Unfortunately, I could not find what language it was supposed to be in (if any). If you know, please let us know.

Flaming brat, page 108

It may seem to the readers that I, as translator, am taking advantage of Natsu's fire magic to add in some fire-based puns to the script. Actually, Japanese uses fire-based descriptive language as well, and whenever the dialogue mentions "burning up," being "on fire," "flaming," etc., there was a Japanese reference to fire in the original line of dialogue.

Finger in the cheek, page 130

Do you know the practical joke of tapping someone on their right shoulder when you stand on their left side (or vice versa) so that they turn to find no one there? This scene represents a common shoulder-tapping joke for the Japanese. You tap a person on the shoulder and point your index finger at their cheek, so in turning toward the tap, they poke their cheek on your immobile finger.

I love my guitar.
Of course, I'm terrible at it, but I
love strumming during breaks in
work...and when I'm stuck as to
what to draw on the *name**.
I just love strumming. Sometimes,
I strum while I work, and I get
the "Yeah, yeah" look from my
staff. You know the look. It's the
"Get back to work" look. Yeah...

—Hiro Mashima

**Name* = A sketched first
draft of a manga.

Honorifics Explained

Throughout the Kodansha Comics books, you will find Japanese honorifics left intact in the translations. For those not familiar with how the Japanese use honorifics and, more important, how they differ from American honorifics, we present this brief overview.

Politeness has always been a critical facet of Japanese culture. Ever since the feudal era, when Japan was a highly stratified society, use of honorifics—which can be defined as polite speech that indicates relationship or status—has played an essential role in the Japanese language. When you address someone in Japanese, an honorific usually takes the form of a suffix attached to one's name (example: "Asuna-san"), is used as a title at the end of one's name, or appears in place of the name itself (example: "Negi-sensei," or simply "Sensei!").

Honorifics can be expressions of respect or endearment. In the context of manga and anime, honorifics give insight into the nature of the relationship between characters. Many English translations leave out these important honorifics and therefore distort the feel of the original Japanese. Because Japanese honorifics contain nuances that English honorifics lack, it is our policy at Kodansha not to translate them. Here, instead, is a guide to some of the honorifics you may encounter in Kodansha Comics.

-san: This is the most common honorific and is equivalent to Mr., Miss, Ms., or Mrs. It is the all-purpose honorific and can be used in any situation where politeness is required.

-sama: This is one level higher than "-san" and is used to confer great respect.

-dono: This comes from the word "tono," which means "lord." It is an even higher level than "-sama" and confers utmost respect.

-kun: This suffix is used at the end of boys' names to express familiarity or endearment. It is also sometimes used by men among friends, or when addressing someone younger or of a lower station.

-chan: This is used to express endearment, mostly toward girls. It is also used for little boys, pets, and even among lovers. It gives a sense of childish cuteness.

Bozu: This is an informal way to refer to a boy, similar to the English terms "kid" and "squirt."

**Sempai/
Senpai:** This title suggests that the addressee is one's senior in a group or organization. It is most often used in a school setting, where underclassmen refer to their upperclassmen as "sempai." It can also be used in the workplace, such as when a newer employee addresses an employee who has seniority in the company.

Kohai: This is the opposite of "sempai" and is used toward underclassmen in school or newcomers in the workplace. It connotes that the addressee is of a lower station.

Sensei: Literally meaning "one who has come before," this title is used for teachers, doctors, or masters of any profession or art.

-[blank]: This is usually forgotten in these lists, but it is perhaps the most significant difference between Japanese and English. The lack of honorific, known as *yobisute*, means that the speaker has permission to address the person in a very intimate way. Usually, only family, spouses, or very close friends have this kind of permission. It can be gratifying when someone who has earned the intimacy starts to call one by one's name without an honorific. But when that intimacy hasn't been earned, it can be very insulting.

Preview of Volume 4

We're pleased to present you with a preview from volume 4,
now available from Kodansha Comics. Check out our Web site
(www.kodanshacomics.com) for more details!

FWOOOO

ヒョォォォォォォ

Natsu! Shut up!

Let me out!!!

Let me out of here!!!

Let me out!!!

......

SHUU

Anyway, change me back!!!

If I let you out, you'd just go on a rampage, right?

I would not!!!

RAAA

This time, she's up against the Council! There's no stopping them.

I would not!! Who would even *want* to save Erza?!!

If I did, the first thing you'd do is scream, "I'm coming to save you!!" Right?

The
Council.
Fiore
Division.

KACLOP

KACLOP

KACLOP

!

Siegrain!!

STPP

My true body is still in Era.

You needn't take such a defensive posture. This body is a thought projection.

ZZT

ZZT

CHANK

FWUMP

Long time no see, Erza.

All of the old farts beyond that door are also thought projections.

No one felt the need to come physically for such a small matter.

I'm mortified... I've stood as Fairy Tail's most ardent defender.

What a farce!

So...this whole thing was a setup by your people?

Ah...No matter. There is only one reason I came to see you prior to the trial.

Shut up!

They want a scapegoat.

They're frantic to dredge up someone they can shunt all the responsibility upon.

But the old farts are all scared that the blame will fall on them.

206